KELSO ABBEY

KELSO ABBEY was founded in 1128, when David I, King of the Scots, brought a group of French monks, whom he had previously settled at Selkirk, to a more suitable site at Kelso just across the river from his castle of Roxburgh. It was the first of four abbeys built in the Borders during his reign. Looking at the shattered fragment that has survived, compared with the more substantial ruins at Jedburgh, Dryburgh and Melrose, it is hard to comprehend that Kelso was at one time the largest and most important of the four Border abbeys and one of the wealthiest in Scotland.

HISTORICAL BACKGROUND

When David I became King in 1124, Scotland as a country was still taking shape. Malcolm II, David's great-great-grandfather, had added Anglo-Saxon-speaking Lothian and Tweeddale to his Gaelic-speaking kingdom of Alba. The Northern and Western Isles were controlled by Norway. However towards the end of his reign, David controlled a large part of what is now Northern England, including Carlisle and the north-west as well as Northumberland. The border between Scotland and England as we know it today was not finally agreed until some hundred years later.

As the youngest son of Malcolm III Canmore (the son of Duncan and enemy of Macbeth in Shakespeare's play) and Margaret, his second wife, David could not have expected to inherit the throne. Margaret was a princess of the English royal family, who, with her brother and other English nobles, had taken refuge in Scotland after the Norman conquest of England by William the Conqueror in 1066. She is credited with being a civilising influence on the Scottish court and brought the first Benedictine monks to Scotland to Dunfermline Abbey, becoming St Margaret after her death. David's sister, Matilda, married Henry I of England, and David's own wife, also Matilda, brought him the Earldom of Huntingdon, wide lands in Northamptonshire and claims to Northumbria. A power struggle between Malcolm's sons after his death in 1093 left David ruling the south of the country as Earl of Cumbria for his brother, Alexander I. When Alexander died without an heir in 1124, David became King of Scotland.

During his long reign (1124-1153) David used the experience he had gained at the Anglo-Norman court to reorganize his Scottish kingdom on similar lines. He consolidated his hold over outlying areas like Moray and Argyll. Sheriffdoms were set up to administer royal authority and he brought a number of his Anglo-Norman friends to Scotland to help him in this task – men like Robert de Brus, Walter FitzAlan (ancestor of the Stewarts), William Comyn and Hugh de Morville, whose military and administrative skills would be used in the King's service. He began the setting up of royal burghs, such as Roxburgh, as centres of trade, which brought in valuable revenues for the Crown. Like his mother and elder brothers, David was deeply religious and played a major part in reorganising the church. Many of Scotland's abbeys and priories date from his reign. His descendant, James I, is reported to have described him as 'a sair sanct for the croun' [a costly saint for the Crown] because of the amount of royal land he gave to the church. It was David, more than anyone else, who created the medieval kingdom of Scotland.

THE FOUNDING OF KELSO ABBEY

For his first major religious foundation David chose to bring to Scotland monks from Thiron in Northern France. It was in 1113 that David (then still Earl of Cumbria) brought a group of thirteen French monks led by Abbot Ralph to Selkirk. The monks were given substantial property – lands in Selkirk, Midlem, Bowden, Eildon, Melrose (later transferred to Melrose Abbey) and Sprouston, as well as properties in the burghs of Roxburgh and Berwick and revenues from property on David's English estates in Northamptonshire. However the site at Selkirk was found to be inconvenient and about 1127 the decision was taken to move the monastery to Kelso, just across the Tweed from Roxburgh. It was endowed further with lands in the vicinity. It is likely that there was already a religious establishment of some kind at Kelso, because the charter from King David says that the monks were given 'the church of the Blessed Virgin Mary on the banks of the Tweed at the place called Calkou'.

By now David was King of the Scots and Roxburgh Castle on the Marchmound between the rivers Tweed and Teviot was one of his major strongholds. Next to his castle he had created the royal burgh of Roxburgh (now the green field containing the point-to-point course) as a centre for trade and economic activity. Indeed Roxburgh at that time can be considered the chief centre of royal power in Scotland – the capital of the kingdom. This explains why David chose Kelso as a much more suitable place for his monks; he wanted to have them close to him. The monks, led by Abbot Herbert their third abbot, moved down the Tweed from Selkirk to Kelso and the new abbey church was consecrated on 3rd May 1128. It was dedicated to the Blessed Virgin Mary and St John.

David's choice of monks from Thiron is interesting as it shows him to be very much at the forefront of thinking on religious matters at that time. The Tironensians were a reformed Benedictine order only recently founded by St Bernard de Abbeville (c1050-1116). The first monastic settlement in the Thiron area had been set up as recently as 1109 and the monks moved to the site of what became the Abbey of Thiron in 1113. Originally St Bernard had been a monk at a Cluniac monastery at Poitiers. However, following a quarrel with the senior members of the order, he left there and for several years lived as a hermit, before founding his own order of monks at Thiron. Bernard and his followers sought a return to the strict observance of the Benedictine rule; a monk's life should be divided between prayer, manual work and the study and contemplation of the divine texts. He should lead a simple ascetic life, wear a plain grey robe and sleep on a straw mattress with one blanket. The Tironensians were noted for the austerity of their life style. They were also noted for their craftsmanship, for from the first the monks were encouraged to use the skills they brought to the abbey in the service of the monastic community.

Presumably David had learned about St Bernard and his ideas during his visits to Normandy in the following of Henry I. It seems that David visited the area of Thiron in 1116 in the hope of meeting St Bernard – unsuccessfully since Bernard

ST BERNARD DE ABBEVILLE (12TH CENTURY FRENCH FRESCO)

had died in April of that year. A major influence on David's thinking was John, his former tutor and chaplain, whom he had made Bishop of Glasgow when he became Earl of Cumbria. The founding charters of the abbey make clear that the King was acting with the advice of John, Bishop of Glasgow, when the move was made to Kelso. John seems to have been closely linked to the Tironensians. Although it is unclear if in fact he was ever a monk at Thiron, he certainly chose it as the place to retire to in 1136-39, when he resigned his see of Glasgow rather than submit to the demands of the Archbishop of York for his oath of obedience (there was a long running dispute about whether or not the jurisdiction of the Archbishop of York included the Scottish bishoprics and for obvious reasons the Scottish kings and the Scottish church resisted all attempts to bring them under the authority of an English Archbishop).

Whatever the influences that led David to chose the Tironensians, there is no doubt of his motives in setting up the Abbey. Like everyone of the period, David believed strongly in the power of prayer to save souls from the terrors of Hell. It was believed that only a few truly saintly people could hope to go directly to Heaven, while the worst sinners went to eternal torment in the pit of Hell. For the rest there was Purgatory, where the dead would suffer due punishment for the sins they had committed during their lives on earth – perhaps for thousands of years – before they could hope to go to Heaven. Prayers said for the souls of the dead by monks dedicated to the religious life had greater force than the prayers of ordinary sinners, and might help to shorten the time spent in Purgatory, so one of the daily tasks of the monks was to pray for the souls of the Abbey's benefactors. David's charter to the monks states that he founded the abbey for the sake of his soul and the soul of his father and mother, his brothers and sisters, and all his ancestors.

However he was thinking not only of his immortal soul. There were also practical benefits to be had from bringing those foreign monks to Scotland for they were educated men who brought with them many useful skills, everything from building and carpentry to the writing of documents and the production of fine books. Monastic estates operating on a larger scale than most other estates were generally well run, and the monks' foreign contacts meant they were in touch with the most up-to-date methods of farming and business. David was anxious to modernise his country and bringing in monks from abroad was one way of doing this.

THE BUILDING OF THE ABBEY

Although the Abbey church was consecrated in May 1128, the construction of the church and other buildings would have taken most of the next one hundred years. Indeed for much of its early history Kelso Abbey must have resembled a building site, the monks housed in temporary structures whilst they, their masons and their workmen laboured on the building of the permanent stone structures. The stone, which seems to have been brought from quarries at Hendersyde to the north of the Tweed and Sprouston on the other side of the river, would have been cut and shaped by hand by skilled masons. Those masons may have been recruited in England or perhaps even further afield. Wooden scaffolding and simple rope pulleys would have been used to raise the stones into place. The east end of the church was the first part to be built; probably it was completed by 1152, because when Prince Henry, David I's son and heir, died that year he was buried in the church at Kelso before the high altar. The remainder of the great church took many more years to complete, being finally dedicated by David de Bernham, Bishop of St Andrews, in March 1243.

It is only the western end of the church that is left standing today. The eastern end probably lay somewhere beyond the Abbey Row Community Centre towards The Knowes car park. Excavations around the Abbey Row Centre in 1971 uncovered some traces of the foundations of the eastern end of the church. More recently, when the building at the corner of the Knowes (originally designed as a public toilet, but now the 'Wee Gallery') was being built, traces of stones from the east end of the church were found. Though we cannot be sure of the full extent of the church, because it suffered such destruction in the 16th century, it must have been a magnificent building.

The abbey church is very unusual, because it was in the shape of a double cross with transepts at the west end as well as the east. Churches of a similar plan are rare in Britain, but have been found in the Rhineland dating from this period. The surviving buildings belong to the 'Transitional' late Romanesque or Norman style, replaced during the 13th century by the Gothic style with its tall pointed arches The rounded arches of Kelso Abbey and the type of decoration used look back to the Romanesque; there is little evidence of the new Gothic architecture, so this fits in well with the late 12th to early 13th century date for the building of the church. However one fine Gothic doorway preserved to the south of the main building hints at what the later buildings of the abbey might have looked like. Clearly the doorway has been moved to its present position from somewhere else; perhaps it was once part of the decorative doorway to the Chapter House, which was the most important building in the abbey after the church itself.

We are fortunate in having a description of Kelso Abbey from the early 16th century, provided by John Duncan, a cleric of Glasgow, which has been preserved in the Vatican records. Duncan tells us:

> The church…has two high chapels on each side, like wings, which give the church the likeness of a double cross. Its fabric is of squared grey stone, and it is very old indeed. It has three doorways, one towards the west in the forepart, and the other two at the sides. It is divided into three naves

by a double row of columns. The entire roof of the church is wooden, and its outer covering is of leaden sheets. The ground within is partly paved with stone and partly floored with bare earth. It has two towers, one at the first entrance to the church, the other in the inner part at the choir; both are square in plan and are crowned by pyramidal roofs…The first contains many sweet sounding bells, the other, at the choir, is empty on account of decay and age. The church is divided by a transverse wall into two parts; the outer part is open to all, especially parishioners both men and women, who there hear masses and receive all sacraments from their parochial vicar. The other part, the back of the church, takes only monks who chant and celebrate the divine office…

The high altar is at the head of the choir facing east, and on this several choral masses are celebrated daily, one for the founder and the others according to the current feast or holy day. There are besides, in the whole church, twelve or thirteen altars on which several masses are said daily…

In the middle of the church, on that wall which divides the monks from the parishioners there is a platform of wood; here stands the altar of the Holy Rood on which the Body of Christ is reserved and assiduously worshipped, and there is great worship and devotion of the parishioners.

For the rest of the abbey buildings we must use our imagination, because they were totally destroyed during the wars of the 16th century. However since all monasteries were built to broadly the same plan, it is not too difficult to work out what has disappeared. To the south of the church, in the area later used as a graveyard, there would have been the Cloister, a large open square with a covered walkway round its edges. Traces of walls found in excavations in 1971 and 1975-76 suggest it was about 30 metres wide. Around the Cloister would be grouped all the main buildings. The Chapter House was the most important building on the east side, where the monks met each day to hear a reading of a chapter of the monastic rules and deal with any matters of discipline. The monks' library and the school-room, where novice monks were educated, also may have been in this wing. Certainly the monks' dormitory would have been on the floor above, linked by a night stair to the east end of the church, to allow the monks to go quickly to the night masses. The south side of the Cloister would have held the kitchen and the refectory or monks' dining room; we are told by Duncan that Kelso had two refectories, a large and a small one. The west side probably contained storage rooms as well as the outer parlour (the only part of the Cloister buildings still in existence), where visitors could come to talk to the monks.

Beyond the main buildings would have been various other structures. Excavations undertaken to the south-east prior to new houses being built revealed the foundations of a large building that was identified as the Infirmary,

AN IMPRESSION OF THE ABBEY BY A F MORSE, BASED ON DETAILS SUPPLIED TO THE VATICAN IN 1517

where the monks tended the sick. Similarly excavations carried out before the building of Rennie Court on the other side of Bridge Street revealed the foundations of buildings that may have been connected with the abbey's Guest House. Duncan tells us there were granaries and other places for storing corn and goods, and also an orchard and garden. The monks' cemetery lay to the north, where the Old Parish Church graveyard succeeded it. The monks were the first to dam the Tweed at Kelso; Hogarth's Mill, which is still a working flour mill, stands on the site of the medieval mill.

Although the monks normally lived their lives apart from the outside world, their presence would bring many benefits to the local population. The west end of the great church was used by the people of Kelso as their parish church. Daily masses would be celebrated here by a secular priest appointed by the monks, whose own services were carried on out of sight behind the screen that divided the church. We know too that the monks ran schools, not only at the abbey but apparently also at Roxburgh, and a hospice to care for the poor and sick at Maisondieu just south-west of Kelso. Like all monastic establishments of the time, the abbey would have been an important source of charity for the poor; one of the monks, the Almoner, would have had the task of handing out food and clothing to poor people at the abbey gate. The monks also provided food and shelter to travellers in their guest house.

Next to the abbey the village of Kelso seems to have prospered. A charter of King William the Lion informs us that the inhabitants were allowed to sell goods in their own market as long as they did not do so on the days when the Roxburgh market was operating, the king being anxious to protect his royal burgh from undue competition. In fact by the end of the 13th century there seems to have been two distinct parts to Kelso, Easter Kelso next to the abbey, probably mainly for abbey servants, and Wester Kelso half a mile further up the Tweed opposite Roxburgh.

MORE ABOUT THE ARCHITECTURE

As has been mentioned, what is left of Kelso Abbey belongs mostly to the late Romanesque or Norman style. Although the west end of the church was not completed until some hundred years after the first foundation, the monks seem to have kept largely to their original design. There is little evidence of the new Gothic style which was beginning to sweep across Western Europe about this time. The great west doorway must have been a magnificent feature judging by what survives. Although it is damaged and eroded by the weather, the north side of the door still stands with its series of recessed arches decorated with various motifs including the nail head, cable and chevron. Above it was probably a large single window. To the left of the door the wall is decorated with blind arcading.

The doorway led into a Galilee porch. Here too the walls are decorated with blind arcading at ground level. Above that are three more levels and it is possible to identify the walkways on each level. The windows are typically in round-arched Romanesque style, as are those in the transepts, but the tall arches at the crossing, which once supported the west tower, are slightly pointed in the Gothic style. The north-east pier has completely vanished. The south transept was railed off in the 19th century as a burial aisle for the Dukes of Roxburgh; it also contains three 14th century burial slabs and in the south wall there are a piscina and an aumbry.

The north door, which would have provided access for the people of the town, also has a recessed archway with some interesting decoration including flowers. Above it is an arcade with five lancet windows in the centre, presumably to allow someone inside to check on the people outside the door; this is topped off with a pediment decorated with a grid pattern. Of the nave only two bays on the south side survive, the simple decoration of the piers no doubt reflecting the austere views of the early monks. Above can be seen a triforium and clerestory. Traces of the vaulting that once covered the south aisle of the church can be made out and the line of the outside wall is now marked with stones. The cloister must have been in the space now occupied by the graveyard, but there is little trace of it apart from a blocked up doorway

THE SOUTH TRANSEPT

covered by the Scott family tomb, which must have been at the north-west corner of the cloister.

Returning to the entrance to the abbey, to the south of the main front can be seen the doorway to the outer parlour, a barrel-vaulted building that led through to the cloister; here monks might be able to speak to visitors. Beyond that is a fine Gothic trefoil-headed doorway dating from the 13th century, which has been moved here from the Chapter House entrance perhaps. It is now incorporated into a memorial 'cloister' built for the Roxburghe family in 1933.

THE ABBEY'S IMPORTANCE DURING THE MIDDLE AGES

In the early middle ages Kelso Abbey was one of the most important and wealthy institutions in Scotland; its abbots were counted among the leading men of the kingdom. However during the later middle ages Kelso suffered increasingly from the effects of the wars that started with the struggle for independence under Wallace and Bruce and continued off and on until the mid-16th century.

Thanks to the generosity of David I, the abbey owned extensive properties in the Borders and elsewhere. As has been mentioned, in addition to Kelso the monks were given lands and property in places across the country such as

Roxburgh, Berwick, Ednam, Sprouston, Redden, Midlem, Bowden, Lilliesleaf, Selkirk and even as far away as Lanark and Renfrew. In addition they were granted other valuable assets – churches, mills and ferries, the revenues from which accrued to the abbey; the right to cut peat or wood in certain places; a salt works; the right to all the fishing between Brokesmouth (somewhere west of Kelso) and Edenmouth; fishing rights in the waters about Selkirk; a tenth of the beasts and swine and cheese from part of the royal lands in Galloway; half the fat of all the whales stranded in the Forth… The list is extensive and varied. It was added to by many lesser donors, such as Earl Gospatrick, who gave them churches and land at Hume and Fogo, and Uctred of Molla, who donated the church and lands at Mow in the Bowmont valley, to give just two examples. The abbey's possessions continued to grow; over the years many laymen, both rich and poor, gave gifts to the abbey in return for the prayers of the monks or the right to be buried in the abbey precincts.

Obviously it was not possible for the monks to work all these lands themselves, so the majority would be rented out. In the early days the rents would have been paid mainly in kind – bags of grain, cheeses, labour to cut and carry peats, etc. As the Scottish economy developed and money circulated more widely, the monks increasingly converted this into money rents. On their lands in the Cheviots the monks had large sheep farms. It is reckoned that at one time they owned some 7,000 sheep. The wool would have been taken to Berwick, one of Scotland's main seaports at the time, to be exported to Europe. A number of the monks' tenants had as part of their rent the obligation to provide a horse and cart to carry goods to Berwick. Clearly the abbey was at the centre of a major commercial enterprise.

In 1144 David I gave Kelso Abbey land at Lesmahagow in the west of Scotland, where a priory dependent on the abbey was founded. Three other Tironensian abbeys were founded in Scotland. In 1162 Hugh de Morville founded the Abbey of Kilwinning. In 1178 King William the Lion set up Arbroath Abbey with a group of monks brought from Kelso. Another daughter house of Kelso was established in 1191 at Lindores in Fife by David, Earl of Huntingdon. Although they owed their origins to Kelso, the three abbeys were independent of the mother house.

The influence of Kelso Abbey in Scotland in the early middle ages was considerable. The Abbots of Kelso were very important men, who might well take part in royal councils. Their status is demonstrated by the fact that in 1147 Abbot Herbert, the first abbot of Kelso, became Bishop of Glasgow, while the second abbot, Arnold, was appointed Bishop of St Andrews in 1160 – two Kelso abbots appointed to the two most important sees in Scotland (it was Arnold who began the building of the cathedral at St Andrews). John, the next abbot, seems to have been an ambitious character. In 1165 he obtained a

ENGRAVING OF THE WEST FRONT C.1850

mitre from the Pope, which gave the Abbot of Kelso equal status with bishops and meant the abbey was answerable only to the Pope. He also claimed precedence over all the other religious houses in Scotland – even over the mother house of the order at Thiron – on account of Kelso's great wealth and size. His successor Osbert went to Rome as part of a Scottish embassy on behalf of King William the Lion. In 1215 Abbot Henry was in Rome to attend the Fourth Lateran Council.

As mentioned previously, David I chose Kelso for the tomb of his only son, Prince Henry, rather than Dunfermline Abbey where other members of the royal family had been buried. No doubt there were other royal visits to the abbey by David and his successors. It is known that in 1256 the young Alexander III and his Queen, Margaret, daughter of King Henry III of England, took part in a royal procession from Roxburgh to Kelso Abbey. However with the death of Alexander III in 1286 and that of his only direct heir, his granddaughter Margaret, Maid of Norway, four years later, Scotland was plunged into the succession crisis that led to the Wars of Independence. Abbot Richard of Kelso supported the claims of John Balliol to the throne, acting as one of his commissioners in 1291. However in 1296 Edward I of England forcibly removed John from the throne and made himself ruler of Scotland. The abbot and monks of Kelso are recorded as having taken the oath of loyalty to Edward in August of that year.

Within a year Scottish resistance to English rule had appeared. First under William Wallace and then under Robert de Bruce the Scots fought to recover their independence. The Scots were victorious against Edward II at Bannockburn in 1314 and finally in 1328 Edward III signed a treaty accepting Robert as King of Scotland. The peace was short lived, however. By 1332 war had broken out again and two years later the situation had got so serious that David II, King Robert's young son, had to be sent to France for safety; with him went his tutor William de Dalgernock, Abbot of Kelso.

The wars with England continued sporadically for over two hundred years with the Borders as the main battle ground. Berwick and Roxburgh both changed hands several times and Berwick finally ended up permanently in English hands. Roxburgh, held by the English for over a hundred years, was eventually recaptured in 1460. James II of Scotland arrived to besiege it with an army equipped with some of the latest technology – cannons. Unfortunately James took too great an interest in his new weapon and, standing next to one when it exploded, was fatally injured. Undaunted, the Scots continued the siege and took and destroyed Roxburgh. The coronation of the new king, James III, who was just eight years old, was held in Kelso Abbey.

Clearly Kelso Abbey, situated just five miles from the English border and close to Roxburgh Castle, suffered badly throughout that turbulent time.

During the Wars of Independence the Bishop of Glasgow reported:
> The Benedictine monastery of St Mary of Calchow which used to show a liberal hospitality to all who crowded thither, and lent a helping hand to the poor and needy, being situated on the confines of the kingdom, through the hostile incursions and long continued wars…is now impoverished, spoiled of its goods and in a sort desolate.

This dismal picture is confirmed by the Bishop of St Andrews, who tells us that the abbey is:
> …through the common war and long depredation of goods by fire and rapine destroyed, and, we speak it with grief, its monks…wander over Scotland, begging food and clothing at the other religious houses…

In 1344 David II granted the monks leave to cut timber in the royal forests of Jedburgh and Selkirk to repair the abbey. At various times during the 14th and 15th century the kings of both England and Scotland issued letters of protection to the abbey, but its location in an area constantly being fought over made it difficult for the abbey to survive.

THE FINAL YEARS OF THE ABBEY

By the end of the 15th century the Roman Catholic Church was in trouble. Where once churchmen had been respected as men of God, there was increasing resentment at the large amount of land and wealth that they controlled. Kings began to use the top offices of the church as a means of providing for members of their family. Younger brothers or illegitimate sons were made bishops or archbishops or they became commendators of abbeys, able to exploit the monastic revenues for their own upkeep. Small wonder that when Martin Luther sparked off the Protestant Reformation in Germany in 1517 his ideas found a ready audience throughout Europe.

Kelso Abbey was in serious decline by this time, but it was still sufficiently wealthy to make it a worthwhile prize. In 1511 James IV gave the Abbey 'in commendam' to Andrew Stewart, Bishop of Caithness; although Andrew was not a monk and could not therefore be abbot, he gained control of the abbey's revenues. In the wake of the defeat at Flodden in 1513 Dand Ker, laird of Ferniehurst, broke into the abbey and installed Thomas, his brother, as abbot. Was this the same abbot of Kelso who was in prison at Dunfermline in 1515? In any event Thomas seems to have continued in office for a number of years thereafter. In 1536 James V's bastard son, James Stewart then aged fourteen, was made commendator of both Kelso and Melrose, a position he enjoyed for over twenty years.

These were years of war and strife on both sides of the Border. The local population, living with the regular threat of invasion, survived largely by reiving or raiding across the Border to steal cattle and anything else they could lay their hands on. After the disaster of Flodden, when James IV was killed with most of his army, relations with England remained hostile. In 1523 the town and abbey of Kelso were burned down by an English force led by Lord Dacre. In 1542 Kelso suffered again, this time at the hands of the Duke of Norfolk. Although the abbey buildings no doubt were damaged, thus far the thick walls of the old Romanesque church had withstood the various assaults. The final destruction came in 1545 as a result of the 'Rough Wooing.'

The 'Rough Wooing' was the wry term applied to the English invasions of 1544-45, when Henry VIII sent his armies north to intimidate the Scots with a display of force into agreeing to marry their infant Queen, Mary, to his son Prince Edward. Most of south-east Scotland between the Border and Edinburgh was laid waste by the English armies, but Henry's plan failed for the Scots defiantly opted to send Mary, Queen of Scots to France, where she was engaged to marry the French Dauphin instead. By this time Henry had become a Protestant, having fallen out with the Pope over his refusal to annul Henry's marriage to Catherine of Aragon. Having declared himself Head of the Church of England, Henry happily closed down the English monasteries and appropriated their wealth to top up the royal treasury. His commander for the invasion force, the Earl of Hertford, was a keen Protestant who had no qualms about wreaking destruction on the Roman Catholic abbeys of Scotland. Kelso was one of his main targets.

In a letter from his camp at Kelso dated 11th September 1545 Hertford reported to Henry that about a hundred Scots had fortified the abbey church against the English army. Hertford used his guns to breach the walls, but the Scots retreated into the tower and refused to surrender. During the night many of them escaped using ropes, but in the morning the attack was renewed, the tower was taken and the remaining Scots were killed. The Earl of Hertford went on to explain to his king that he had considered fortifying Kelso Abbey as an English base, but after some discussion with his masons he had given up the idea. It appeared there would have been too much work involved in clearing superfluous buildings 'of gret height and circuit' and in any case there was a danger of being cut off from England when the Tweed flooded. Hertford decided therefore 'to rase and deface the house of Kelso, so as th'enenmye shal have lytell commoditie of the same …' Clearly Hertford carried out his plan to the full, because most of the abbey seems to have been razed to the ground, presumably using gunpowder to undermine the walls. Only the west end of the church survived, perhaps spared because it was used by the townspeople as their parish church.

Several of the monks returned to their ruined home, but little could be done to repair the damage before the final episode in the abbey's long history. Protestantism had been spreading rapidly in Scotland and in 1560 it became the official religion of the country. Around this time a Protestant mob burst into the abbey, drove out the few remaining monks and destroyed its statues

KELSO ABBEY BY JOHN SLEZER c.1684
THE VIEW SHOWS THE EXTENT OF ITS REBUILDING FOR USE AS THE PARISH CHURCH
AND THE SUBSEQUENT ADDITION OF A SCHOOL BUILDING IN THE SEVENTEENTH CENTURY

and images. An Act of Parliament in 1587 declared that 'the haill monkis of the abbay of Kelso ar decessit'. After over 400 years Kelso Abbey had ceased to exist.

THE ABBEY SINCE THE REFORMATION

The only part of the Abbey to survive the devastation of 1545 was the west end of the great church. It continued to be used as the parish church of Kelso until the late 18th century, a wall being built across the east side of the transept to close it off. The tumbled stones from the rest of the abbey ruins were carted off to be used in a multitude of building work elsewhere. No doubt most of Kelso's older houses and boundary walls were constructed using abbey stone; why go to the trouble of quarrying stone when it is lying around for the taking? A chamber above the church was used for a time as the town's prison, and a parish school was constructed in what had been the nave of the abbey church. In 1771 it was decided to build a new parish church. According to local tradition there had been a fall of plaster from the ceiling of the church in the abbey ruins and this caused great alarm since it was recalled that there was an ancient prophecy that Kelso's church would fall when it was at its fullest. Built on the other side of the church yard to a design by James Nisbet, the new parish church was completed in 1773 and the abbey was abandoned.

After the Reformation the abbey was held by two commendators, Sir John Maitland and Francis Stewart, Earl of Bothwell. In 1599 a large part of the property of the abbey, including all the Kelso area and also the site of the destroyed town and castle of Roxburgh, was given by King James VI to Sir Robert Ker of Cessford, who took the title of Lord Roxburgh. In 1866 one of his descendants, the Duke of Roxburghe, repaired what little was left of the abbey and the south transept was put into use as the Roxburghe family burial ground. In 1933 a memorial in the form of a cloister was built on the south side of the abbey in honour of the 8th Duke of Roxburghe, which is still used for family burials. The rest of the building was handed over to Historic Scotland and remains in its care today.

GOTHIC DOORWAY, POSSIBLY FROM THE CHAPTER HOUSE, WITH THE ROXBURGHE MEMORIAL CLOISTER BEYOND

First published in Great Britain in 2010 and reprinted with minor amendments in 2014 by Friends of Kelso Museum, 9 Abbey Row, Kelso TD5 7JF
ISBN: 978-0-9563397-2-0

Text and colour photographs of abbey © Christine Henderson
Photograph of St Bernard fresco © Denis Guillemin

Designed and typeset in Optima LT by Bill Smith
Printed in Scotland by Footeprint